# QUIZPEDIA

## AISLING COUGHLAN

# MOVIES

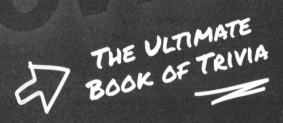

THE ULTIMATE BOOK of TRIVIA

Smith Street Books

# SO YOU THINK
# YOU KNOW ...

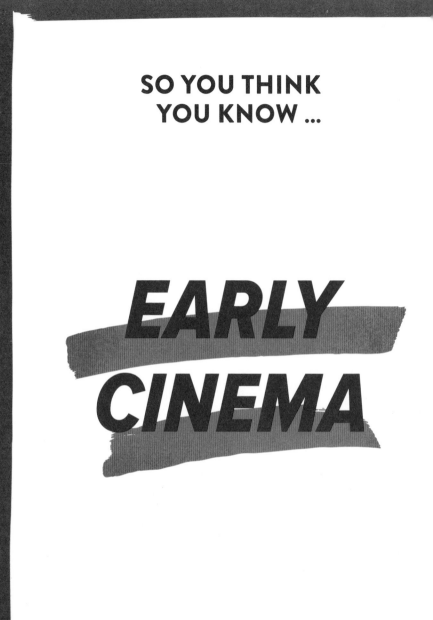

# EARLY
# CINEMA

# Quiz 01

**1.**
Which French brothers were the first to show moving pictures on screen in 1895?

**2.**
Who directed the 1927 sci-fi classic *Metropolis*?

**3.**
Was *The Wizard of Oz* the first feature film to be shown in color?

**4.**
The stage name of which golden age of Hollywood star, whose given name was Lucille LeSueur, was decided by a magazine competition?

**5.**
The first Australian feature-length film, made in 1906, was about which notorious group of outlaws?

**6.**
The Tramp is the on-screen persona of which silent film star?

**7.**
What was Disney's first feature-length animation film?

**8.**
The first Cannes Film Festival was held in which decade?

**9.**
MGM, Paramount Pictures, RKO, 20th Century Fox and Warner Bros. dominated the US movie business from the 1930s to the 1960s – by what name were they collectively known?

**10.**
True or false: The Hollywood sign once read Hollywoodland?

# SO YOU THINK YOU KNOW ...

# MOB MOVIES

I'M GOING TO MAKE HIM AN OFFER HE CAN'T REFUSE

# Quiz 02

**1.**
The Corleone family are characters in which gangster trilogy?

**2.**
Kevin Costner plays Eliot Ness on a mission to bring down Al Capone in which 1987 movie?

**3.**
Which 2019 movie saw the lead characters heavily digitally de-aged?

**4.**
*The Many Saints of Newark* is a prequel to TV hit *The Sopranos*. What's notable about the lead actors of both productions?

**5.**
Which two Oscar-winning actors go head-to-head in *American Gangster*?

**6.**
Which 1990 classic is based on real-life gangster turned informant Henry Hill?

**7.**
Which movie, starring Robert De Niro, was the last that Sergio Leone directed?

**8.**
Which black-and-white classic gave us the famous line, "I coulda been a contender"?

**9.**
Which actress plays a mafia widow in *Married to the Mob*?

**10.**
Tom Hardy played which real-life brothers in *Legend*?

SO YOU THINK
YOU KNOW ...

# HEROES AND VILLAINS

# Quiz 03

**1.**
Tim Burton, Joel Schumacher and Christopher Nolan have all directed movies about which tormented hero?

**2.**
Blue-skinned shapeshifter Mystique is from which franchise?

**3.**
Which superhero shares his name with a popular music app?

**4.**
In *The Wizard of Oz*, who did Dorothy kill with her house?

**5.**
Fictional character Arthur Fleck, failed comedian, is better known by what other name?

**6.**
Which anti-hero files the horns that grow from his head?

**7.**
Zoë Kravitz and Michelle Pfeiffer have both played which role?

**8.**
Who played Lex Luthor to Christopher Reeve's Superman in the 1978 movie?

**9.**
Angelina Jolie donned cheek implants to play which villain?

**10.**
Which aspiring musician battles his girlfriend's seven evil superpowered ex-boyfriends?

# SO YOU THINK YOU KNOW ...

ROM COMS

# Quiz 04

**1.**
*Joe Verses the Volcano*, *You've Got Mail* and *Sleepless in Seattle* saw the pairing of which two actors?

**2.**
What affliction does Lucy, played by Drew Barrymore, have in *50 First Dates*?

**3.**
To where did Shirley Valentine escape to get away from her dreary life?

**4.**
Cher won a Best Actress Oscar for her performance in which 1987 rom com?

**5.**
Hugh Grant stars as cad Daniel Cleaver in which movie series?

**6.**
Keanu Reeves plays Ali Wong's on-screen love interest in which movie about childhood sweethearts?

**7.**
Dudley Moore falls for a cornrow-sporting Bo Derek in which 70s movie?

**8.**
Which actor played Toula's love interest in *My Big Fat Greek Wedding*?

**9.**
What is Hitch's job in the movie of the same name?

**10.**
Julia Roberts and Richard Gere played opposite each other in which two movies?

# SO YOU THINK
# YOU KNOW ...

# *MOVIE*

# *MUSIC*

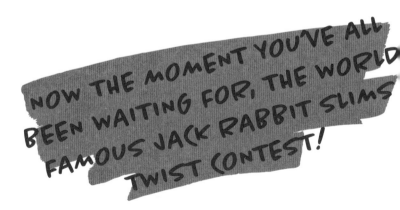

NOW THE MOMENT YOU'VE ALL BEEN WAITING FOR, THE WORLD FAMOUS JACK RABBIT SLIMS TWIST CONTEST!

# Quiz 05

**1.**
To which Chuck Berry song did Mia Wallace and Vincent Vega twist to in *Pulp Fiction*?

**2.**
Which prolific composer wrote the score for *The Mission*?

**3.**
Public Enemy's "Fight the Power" was written for what 1989 movie?

**4.**
Who composed the music for *Jaws* and the Star Wars franchise?

**5.**
Who wrote "I Will Always Love You," a hit for Whitney Houston from the soundtrack to *The Bodyguard*?

**6.**
What song is playing under Ewan McGregor's "Choose life" speech in *Trainspotting*?

**7.**
The Bee Gees provided the soundtrack for which disco classic?

**8.**
John Legend and Common won Oscars for their song "Glory" from which movie about civil rights?

**9.**
Beethoven and extreme violence are paired together in which Stanley Kubrick movie?

**10.**
What song was a hit for Eminem from the semi-autobiographical *8 Mile*?

# SO YOU THINK
# YOU KNOW ...

# Quiz 06

**1.**
True or false: The 2021 movie *Dune* is a sequel to the 1984 David Lynch movie of the same name?

**2.**
Which is the only movie in the Alien franchise that doesn't feature the word "Alien"?

**3.**
Who plays the president in *Independence Day*?

**4.**
Which movie's plot includes a small silver spinning top that tells its owner if he's awake or asleep?

**5.**
Who wrote the book on which the movie *The War of the Worlds* is based?

**6.**
In which years were the original *Blade Runner* and its 2017 sequel set?

**7.**
Swallowing which color pill will allow you to see the truth about the world in *The Matrix*: red or blue?

**8.**
Which actor portrays chimpanzee Caesar in the reboot of the Planet of the Apes franchise?

**9.**
A software engineer sucked into the digital world is the premise of which 1982 movie?

**10.**
Which two time travelers wrote a song that saved the universe?

# SO YOU THINK
# YOU KNOW ...

# *BOOKS*

# *ON*

# *SCREEN*

# Quiz 07

**1.**
*Capote*, the biographical movie about Truman Capote, is set against the backdrop of the author writing which book?

**2.**
What country is the setting for novel-turned-movie *Call Me By Your Name*?

**3.**
Who wrote the book *Gone with the Wind*?

**4.**
Oprah Winfrey won an Oscar for her performance in which movie based on an Alice Walker novel?

**5.**
Carey Mulligan made her film debut in an adaptation of which Jane Austen book?

**6.**
Aside from a candle flame, what is the only other color used in the black-and-white screen adaptation of Thomas Keneally's *Schindler's List*?

**7.**
Who wrote the short story that inspired *The Shawshank Redemption*?

**8.**
Solomon Northup wrote which 1853 memoir that was the basis of a 2013 movie?

**9.**
Which author wrote the books *Jurassic Park*, *Disclosure* and *Congo*?

**10.**
Harper Lee's creation Atticus Finch is from what book, later a movie of the same name?

# SO YOU THINK
# YOU KNOW ...

# *ANIMATION*

THAT'LL DO, DONKEY,
THAT'LL DO.

# Quiz 08

**1.**
Wes Anderson directed George Clooney and Meryl Streep as husband and wife in which movie?

**2.**
Which pro baller won an Oscar for his short film *Dear Basketball* in 2018?

**3.**
What food does Shrek compare ogres to, when talking to Donkey?

**4.**
Louis Prima provided the voice for which *Jungle Book* character?

**5.**
Which of the sisters in *Frozen* has a magic gift?

**6.**
Hand-drawn animated fantasy *Spirited Away* is from which country?

**7.**
How many movies are in the Toy Story franchise?

**8.**
Which animated musical features the underwater inhabitants of Pepperland?

**9.**
Who is the protagonist of *The Nightmare Before Christmas*?

**10.**
*An American Tail* sees mouse Fievel alone in which city?

# SO YOU THINK YOU KNOW ...

# MOVIE CAMEOS

# Quiz 09

**1.**
Which businessman-come-politician does Kevin McCallister run into in *Home Alone 2*?

**2.**
Horror master Wes Craven cameos as a janitor in his 1996 movie *Scream*. What is he wearing?

**3.**
What rocker inspired the look of Jack Sparrow and had a cameo in the Pirates of the Caribbean franchise?

**4.**
Who had a cameo in every Marvel universe movie, 22 in total, since 2008 until their death in 2018?

**5.**
Who appears chomping on a carrot in the first *Lord of the Rings* movie?

**6.**
Which boy band shows up to make Heaven complete at the end of *This Is the End*?

**7.**
Author of *Jaws*, Peter Benchley, has a cameo as what in the movie version?

**8.**
Which female actor dons a pirate outfit complete with beard and gets sent to the Boo Box in *Hook*?

**9.**
Which Beatle had a brief on-screen moment in *Monty Python's Life of Brian*, and also helped fund the movie?

**10.**
Which music icon moderates a walk-off between Zoolander and Hansel?

# SO YOU THINK YOU KNOW ...

# SHAKESPEARE
# ON SCREEN

# Quiz 10

**1.**
Keanu Reeves plays Denzel Washington's scheming half-brother in which on-screen adaptation?

**2.**
Which actress cried her way through her Best Actress Oscar acceptance speech, having won for playing Shakespeare's love interest in a 1998 movie?

**3.**
Where is Baz Luhrmann's *Romeo + Juliet* set?

**4.**
*The Lion King* is based on which play?

**5.**
Who directed *My Own Private Idaho*, which was inspired by Shakespeare's Henry plays?

**6.**
Japanese movie *Throne of Blood*, about a samurai warrior and his scheming wife, is an interpretation of which play?

**7.**
*10 Things I Hate About You* is an adaptation of which Shakespeare comedy?

**8.**
Which thespian played the title role in *Prospero's Books*?

**9.**
Marlon Brando played which Roman general in 1953's *Julius Caesar*?

**10.**
What's the notable difference between the ending of the play *Romeo and Juliet* and the musical version, *West Side Story*?

# SO YOU THINK
# YOU KNOW ...

# *VAMPIRE*

# *FLICKS*

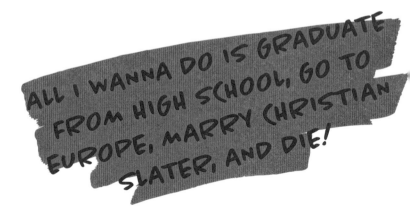

ALL I WANNA DO IS GRADUATE FROM HIGH SCHOOL, GO TO EUROPE, MARRY CHRISTIAN SLATER, AND DIE!

# Quiz 11

**1.**
What was the name of the original screen vampire, seen in 1922's *Nosferatu*?

**2.**
Gary Oldman's version of Dracula has a fondness for licking what?

**3.**
Name the sequel to 1972's Blaxploitation horror film *Blacula*?

**4.**
Kiefer Sutherland stars as the motorbike-riding bleached-blond vampire in which 1987 classic?

**5.**
Which 2008 Swedish movie, based on a book of the same name, is about a 12-year-old boy who forms a friendship with the seemingly normal but very pale girl next door?

**6.**
Which 1990s teen heartthrob played Buffy's love interest in the *Buffy the Vampire Slayer* movie?

**7.**
Which 2003 vampire action movie stars Kate Beckinsale battling lycans, a breed of werewolf?

**8.**
Whose last film role was as the title role in *Queen of the Damned*, based on an Anne Rice novel?

**9.**
What characteristic do the vampires in the Twilight universe have when they step into the sunlight?

**10.**
Who got their breakout role as young vamp Claudia in *Interview with the Vampire*?

# SO YOU THINK
# YOU KNOW ...

# DOCUMENTARIES

# Quiz 12

**1.**
Morgan Spurlock ate only what for the subject of his doco *Super Size Me*?

**2.**
Which 1996 doco chronicled the heavyweight bout dubbed the "Rumble in the Jungle"?

**3.**
Who narrated *March of the Penguins*?

**4.**
Which documentary was about the underground drag ball culture in 1980s New York City?

**5.**
A highwire walk between which two buildings is the subject of *Man on Wire*?

**6.**
Sixto Rodriguez is the focus of which 2012 documentary?

**7.**
Which documentary maker brought us *Bowling for Columbine*?

**8.**
Which former US politician wrote *An Inconvenient Truth*?

**9.**
*Heart of Darkness* is the name of the doco about the making of which movie?

**10.**
Artist Banksy is the subject of what documentary?

# SO YOU THINK YOU KNOW ...

# FAMOUS

## MOVIE

## LOCATIONS

# Quiz 13

**1.**
The beach at the end of *Point Break*, said to be Bells Beach in Australia, was actually which beach?

**2.**
In what famous New York deli did Meg Ryan show us what "faking it" looks like?

**3.**
What country was *Mad Max: Fury Road* filmed in, because Australia had too much rainfall resulting in a too green landscape?

**4.**
Which New York landmark is reportedly the most filmed location in the world?

**5.**
The rocky island of Skellig Michael, off the coast of Ireland, was used in which blockbuster series?

**6.**
Which real country is home to Middle Earth?

**7.**
The success of Danny Boyle's *The Beach* saw increased tourism in which Asian country?

**8.**
Aside from a few scenes filmed in the US, what country was the primary location of Tatooine, Luke Skywalker's home planet?

**9.**
Fox Plaza, the real name of *Die Hard*'s Nakatomi Plaza, is located in which US city?

**10.**
The steps of which building does Rocky run up and down in the 1976 film?

# SO YOU THINK
# YOU KNOW ...

# THRILLERS

## A CENSUS TAKER ONCE TRIED TO TEST ME ...

# Quiz 14

**1.**
Name the five movies that have all featured Thomas Harris's creation Hannibal Lecter?

**2.**
Dr. Richard Kimble hunts the man who killed his wife in which movie?

**3.**
*What Ever Happened to Baby Jane* starred which two real-life feuding leading ladies?

**4.**
Who is Keyser Söze's alias?

**5.**
What tale of survival sees four men canoeing down a river in northern Georgia only to meet some unsettling locals?

**6.**
In which movie do Bridget Fonda and Jennifer Jason Leigh star as roommates gone wrong?

**7.**
Ben Affleck and Rosamund Pike play husband and wife in which thriller?

**8.**
What does Alex, played by Glenn Close, cook up in *Fatal Attraction*?

**9.**
How does Annie (Kathy Bates) prevent Paul (James Caan) from leaving her house in *Misery*?

**10.**
Who wrote and directed *Old*, about a beach where young people age rapidly?

SO YOU THINK
YOU KNOW ...

# WHICH MOVIES
# THESE FAMOUS
# QUOTES COME
# FROM

# Quiz 15

**1.**
"I don't want to survive,
I want to live."

**2.**
"You're gonna need
a bigger boat."

**3.**
"Do or do not, there
is no try."

**4.**
"There's no crying
in baseball."

**5.**
"I have nipples, Greg,
can you milk me?"

**6.**
"That's so fetch."

**7.**
"Rosebud."

**8.**
"You remind me of
the babe."

**9.**
"Exercise gives you
endorphins. Endorphins
make you happy. Happy
people just don't shoot
their husbands."

**10.**
"Every time a bell rings,
an angel gets his wings."

## SO YOU THINK
## YOU KNOW ...

# CREATURES

# AND

# MONSTERS

# Quiz 16

**1.**
Prehistoric sea monster Godzilla is awakened by what external event?

**2.**
What's the most important thing to remember when looking after a mogwai in the movie *Gremlins*?

**3.**
Name the creature from Boon Joon-ho's 2006 film that was released internationally as *The Host*?

**4.**
What creature gets the better of Gandalf the Grey?

**5.**
With red eyes, rows of sharp teeth and a taste for human flesh, what are Krites better known as?

**6.**
The Pale Man from *Pan's Labyrinth* feeds on what?

**7.**
Robert De Niro played what misunderstood literary (and often misnamed) monster?

**8.**
The amphibious Gill-man first appeared in what black-and-white monster movie?

**9.**
What couldn't you do if you didn't want to be killed by a Death Angel in *A Quiet Place*?

**10.**
Name the famous monster movie that contains the famous line "It was beauty killed the beast"?

# *FOOD AND
DRINK ON
SCREEN*

THE DUDE ABIDES

# Quiz 17

**1.**
What's the surprise in Snake Surprise, a dish served in *Indiana Jones and the Temple of Doom*?

**2.**
To which country does Julia Roberts go to eat, in *Eat Pray Love*?

**3.**
What's Jeffrey "The Dude" Lebowski's drink of choice?

**4.**
What was Bruce Bogtrotter forced to eat by wicked Mrs Trunchbull in *Matilda*?

**5.**
What is Bill Murray's character in *Lost in Translation* in Japan to advertise?

**6.**
What does Violet Beauregarde eat that makes her blow up like a balloon in *Willy Wonka's Chocolate Factory*?

**7.**
What kind of sandwich does the food truck from *Chef* dish up?

**8.**
What breakfast dish ends up all over Sarah Jessica Parker on Christmas morning in *The Family Stone*?

**9.**
What was the speciality of the Whistlestop Cafe?

**10.**
According to Hannibal Lecter, what pairs well with human liver?

# SO YOU THINK
# YOU KNOW ...

# MARVEL
# CINEMATIC
# UNIVERSE

# Quiz 18

**1.**
What was the first movie in the Marvel Cinematic Universe, and when was it released?

**2.**
What is Black Panther's real name?

**3.**
For what reason is Steven Rogers bio-engineered into Captain America?

**4.**
What does the acronym S.H.I.E.L.D. stand for?

**5.**
Elizabeth Olsen and Paul Bettany play which Marvel couple?

**6.**
Are Thor and Loki biological brothers?

**7.**
True or False: Bradley Cooper voices Groot in *Guardians of the Galaxy*?

**8.**
In which movie does Thanos first appear?

**9.**
What was the earthly profession of Dr. Stephen Strange, aka Dr. Strange?

**10.**
Who plays Xu Shang-Chi/Shaun in *Shang-Chi and the Legend of the Ten Rings*?

# SO YOU THINK YOU KNOW ...

# SPORTING MOVIES

# Quiz 19

**1.**
What relation is Adonis Creed to Rocky Balboa?

**2.**
*King Richard* is a biopic about the father of which sporting stars?

**3.**
Which movies tells the true story of Eric Liddell and Harold Abrahams, who competed for Britain in the 1924 Olympics?

**4.**
Allison Janney won an Oscar for playing which sports star's mother?

**5.**
The tagline to *Field of Dreams* is: "If you build it, they will come." What is being built and who are "they"?

**6.**
What did the team name their bobsled in *Cool Runnings*?

**7.**
*Ride Like a Girl* is based on Michelle Payne, the first female jockey to win which multi-million dollar horse race?

**8.**
Which movie tells the story of professional boxer Jake LaMotta?

**9.**
*Battle of the Sexes* is based around a tennis match between Bobby Riggs and which tennis champion?

**10.**
Drew Barrymore's directorial debut was about which sport?

# SO YOU THINK YOU KNOW ...

# COMEDY

# HORROR

THE NEIGHBOURS CAN SEE YOU FLYING AROUND THE HOUSE!

# Quiz 20

**1.**
Which two famous New Zealanders wrote, directed and starred in the vampire comedy *What We Do in the Shadows*?

**2.**
Megan Fox stars as the demon-possessed hot girl in school in which movie?

**3.**
Name the slasher movie parody that starred brothers Marlon and Shawn Wayans?

**4.**
Where do the voices come from that Jim, played by Ryan Reynolds, hears that inspire him to kill?

**5.**
Which actress had her first movie speaking role in *Leprechaun*?

**6.**
What movie, which shares its title with a Fleetwood Mac song, features Justin Long and a walrus?

**7.**
What kind of plant is the blood-eating star of *Little Shop of Horrors*?

**8.**
Which Tim Burton movie stars Geena Davis and Alec Baldwin as ghosts?

**9.**
In which movie does Alison Lohman star as a loans officer who is cursed after evicting an old woman?

**10.**
In what movie does a college student find herself reliving her birthday on a loop, being murdered every time?

# SO YOU THINK YOU KNOW ...

# THE

# BECHDEL

# TEST

# Quiz 21

**1.**
What's the basic requirement for a work of fiction to pass the Bechdel test?

**2.**
True or false: You'll find "Bechdel Test" in most major English language dictionaries?

**3.**
Name the person who invented the Bechdel test?

**4.**
The test's creator guest-starred partaking in a panel called "Chicks with Pix" in which TV show?

**5.**
An "A" rating in which country indicates that a movie has passed the test?

**6.**
A blue convertible flying through the air is an image from which Bechdel-passing movie?

**7.**
In what format did the test concept first appear?

**8.**
In what year did it first appear?

**9.**
The Lord of the Rings trilogy features a few strong female characters, but why did it fail the test?

**10.**
Which of these failed the Bechdel test – *A Star Is Born*, *Toy Story*, *La La Land*?

# SO YOU THINK
# YOU KNOW ...

# Quiz 22

**1.**
What match-making movie, starring Meryl Streep, features the songs of ABBA?

**2.**
Danny Zuko and Sandy Olsson are teens in love in what movie?

**3.**
Billy Porter played what role in 2021's *Cinderella*?

**4.**
How many von Trapp children are there in *The Sound of Music*?

**5.**
The Kit Kat Club is the focus of which musical?

**6.**
Yul Brynner stars as the king of which country in *The King and I*?

**7.**
Who wrote *In the Heights*?

**8.**
Mitzi Gaynor sang about washing a man right out of her hair in which musical?

**9.**
The play *Pygmalion* by George Bernard Shaw was remade for the silver screen as which musical?

**10.**
Who played Matron "Mama" Morton in the 2002 version of *Chicago*?

# SO YOU THINK
# YOU KNOW ...

# HITCHCOCK
# CLASSICS

# Quiz 23

**1.**
In which movie does James Stewart play a photographer turned peeping tom?

**2.**
Movies *The Birds*, *Rebecca* and *Jamaica Inn* are all based on books by which author?

**3.**
Who starred as Norman Bates in *Psycho*?

**4.**
Who played the thief in *To Catch a Thief*?

**5.**
What was the name of the 1998 remake of *Dial M for Murder*, starring Michael Douglas, Gwyneth Paltrow and Viggo Mortensen?

**6.**
Alfred Hitchcock was known as the Master of what?

**7.**
Which of his movies was made to look like it was shot in one long take?

**8.**
In *Vertigo*, John "Scottie" Ferguson rescues Madeleine from the water in front of which famous US landmark?

**9.**
Which actress plays Melanie, who faces terror from the sky in *The Birds*?

**10.**
In how many Hitchcock movies did Grace Kelly star?

# SO YOU THINK
# YOU KNOW ...

# *THE*

# *OSCARS*

AND THE OSCAR
GOES TO ...

# Quiz 24

**1.**
The first award was given out in 1929, but when were the Academy Awards first broadcast on TV?

**2.**
Who won the Best Film Oscar in 2017 – *Moonlight* or *La La Land*?

**3.**
Glenn Close and Peter O'Toole share what Oscars-related record?

**4.**
What did Björk leave on the red carpet at the 2001 awards ceremony?

**5.**
On whose behalf did Sacheen Littlefeather refuse a Best Actor award in 1973?

**6.**
What was the first non-English language movie to win Best Picture?

**7.**
For three consecutive years the statues were made of painted plaster, owing to what world event?

**8.**
Which three movies hold the record for having won the most awards (11)?

**9.**
Who was the first woman to win Best Director – and when and for what?

**10.**
Who holds the record for hosting, having done so a whopping 19 times?

# SO YOU THINK YOU KNOW ...

# WITCHES AND WIZARDS

# Quiz 25

**1.**
Who plays Jadis the White Witch in *The Chronicles of Narnia*?

**2.**
What is Lord Voldemort's real (full) name?

**3.**
Nancy, Bonnie, Rochelle and Sarah make up the coven in which teen movie?

**4.**
In which feature-length film did Mickey Mouse star as The Sorcerer's Apprentice?

**5.**
Shadowfax is the horse of which famous wizard?

**6.**
Helen Mirren played Morgana in which Arthurian movie from 1981?

**7.**
Sandra Bullock and Nicole Kidman play witchy sisters in which movie?

**8.**
What kind of animal can Harry Potter speak to?

**9.**
The plot of which comedy involves three scheming Salem witches brought back to life on Halloween?

**10.**
How many witches do we see on screen in *The Wizard of Oz*?

# SO YOU THINK
# YOU KNOW ...

# FASHION
# IN FILM

# Quiz 26

**1.**
Which haute-couture fashion designer created the outlandish costumes for *The Fifth Element*?

**2.**
What pattern dress does Dorothy pair with her ruby slippers?

**3.**
*A Single Man* was directed by which fashion designer?

**4.**
In which 1955 movie is Marilyn Monroe pictured in a white dress above a subway grate?

**5.**
A bright yellow plaid suit is synonymous with which 90s comedy?

**6.**
What color dress did Vivian wear to the opera in *Pretty Woman*?

**7.**
Which movie saw a group of men on a terror spree, dressed all in white with black bowler hats?

**8.**
Which Bond girl emerged from the sea in an orange bikini complete with knife belt and large knife?

**9.**
What color is the dress Scarlett O'Hara makes out of her own curtains?

**10.**
Miranda Priestly from *The Devil Wears Prada* is said to be based on whom?

# *BIOPICS*

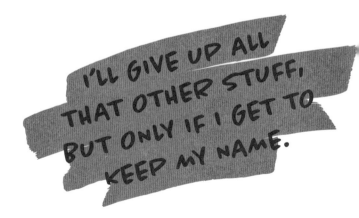

I'LL GIVE UP ALL THAT OTHER STUFF, BUT ONLY IF I GET TO KEEP MY NAME.

# Quiz 27

**1.**
Who played Ike and Tina Turner in 1993's *What's Love Got to Do with It*?

**2.**
O'Shea Jackson Jr. plays his real-life father in which 2015 biopic?

**3.**
In which movie does Daniel Day-Lewis portray Christy Brown, an artist with cerebral palsy?

**4.**
Rami Malek wore false teeth to portray which famous musician?

**5.**
Sean Penn portrayed which openly gay activist and politician in 1970s California?

**6.**
*On the Basis of Sex* charts the rise of which iconic woman?

**7.**
What syndrome is at the centre of *The Diving Bell and The Butterfly*?

**8.**
*Hidden Figures* is about three women who worked where?

**9.**
An abandoned green-and-white bus in the Alaskan wilderness, dubbed The Magic Bus, became a hiking destination after being featured in which biopic?

**10.**
Who portrayed Billie Holiday in 1972's *Lady Sings the Blues*?

# SO YOU THINK YOU KNOW ...

# Quiz 28

**1.**
In what year was the first Star Wars movie released?

**2.**
What planet is Yoda from?

**3.**
What aircraft do the forces of Rebel Alliance fly?

**4.**
How many of the nine Star Wars movies did George Lucas direct?

**5.**
What two actors play a young and older Lando Calrissian in the universe?

**6.**
Who cuts off Luke's hand?

**7.**
Who is Rey's grandfather and ultimate foe?

**8.**
Which character from the original trilogy appears at the end of spin-off *Rogue One*?

**9.**
Who are Luke and Leia's parents?

**10.**
What species of forest dwellers live on the Moon of Endor?

# SO YOU THINK
# YOU KNOW ...

# Quiz 29

**1.**
Pal was the first canine actor to portray which famous on-screen dog?

**2.**
Which movie porker thought he was a dog?

**3.**
Which three actors have played Dr. Dolittle on the big screen?

**4.**
What do Jennifer Lopez's and Ice Cube's characters encounter while filming a documentary in the Amazon rainforest?

**5.**
What is the name of Harry Potter's owl?

**6.**
What movie is about a boy trying to release his friend Keiko back into the wild?

**7.**
What four animals are on the boat with Pi?

**8.**
What kind of dog was Marley?

**9.**
What are the unwelcome traveling companions of FBI agent Neville Flynn (played by Samuel L. Jackson)?

**10.**
What name for a fear of spiders is the title of a 90s thriller?

# SO YOU THINK
# YOU KNOW ...

# SLASHER

# Quiz 30

**1.**
Which slashing ghost haunted the dreams of teens and had his own nursery rhyme?

**2.**
The mask that Michael Myers wears, from the Halloween movies, was made using a cast of which actor's face?

**3.**
What is the profession of Gale Weathers (played by Courteney Cox) in the Scream franchise?

**4.**
What 1979 movie features a phone call, urging the babysitter to check the children?

**5.**
What brand of doll is Chucky?

**6.**
What was the weapon of choice for the vengeful fisherman in *I Know What You Did Last Summer*?

**7.**
A young boy, supposedly accidentally drowned at Camp Crystal Lake, is the event that led to which 12-film franchise?

**8.**
Leatherface, loosely based on serial killer Ed Gein, is the villain in which movie?

**9.**
Which two slasher icons starred in a crossover 2003 movie?

**10.**
Which 1982 movie, remade in 2021, features a drill-wielding maniac?

# SET IN SPACE

THE UNITED STATES GOVERNMENT JUST ASKED US TO SAVE THE WORLD. ANYBODY WANT TO SAY NO?

# Quiz 31

**1.**
What food does Matt Damon's character grow while stranded on Mars in *The Martian*?

**2.**
Ron Howard directed which movie about a failed mission to walk on the moon?

**3.**
Sam Rockwell appears alongside himself in which space movie?

**4.**
Which 1987 space parody starred John Candy, Mel Brooks and Rick Moranis?

**5.**
"In space, no one can hear you scream" is the tagline from which famous space thriller?

**6.**
In the rebooted Star Trek movies, who plays Khan?

**7.**
Before they headed into space to save the world in *Armageddon*, what did Harry Stamper (Bruce Willis) and his team do for a day job?

**8.**
Sandra Bullock crash-lands back to earth solo at the end of which movie?

**9.**
Which sci-fi movie was based on a novel written by Carl Sagan?

**10.**
True or false: Over half of *2001: A Space Odyssey* has no dialogue?

# SO YOU THINK
# YOU KNOW ...

# SPIES AND

# ASSASSINS

# Quiz 32

**1.**
Who were the first six actors to play James Bond?

**2.**
What is the name of the morbidly obese Scottish man who serves Dr. Evil in the Austin Powers movies?

**3.**
Name the James Bond spoof character played by Rowan Atkinson.

**4.**
What is the name of the child assassin played by Saoirse Ronan, in a movie of the same name?

**5.**
Real-life covert mission termed the "Canadian Caper" was the inspiration for which Oscar-winning movie?

**6.**
Who directed the 2015 reboot of the 60s TV series *The Man from U.N.C.L.E.*?

**7.**
Gary "Eggsy" Unwin is a member of which fictional spy agency?

**8.**
How does the Bride kill Bill?

**9.**
Angelina Jolie stars as a CIA agent on the run after being accused of being a Russian spy in which movie?

**10.**
Which French 1990 movie, named for its criminal-turned-government assassin, was directed by Luc Besson?

# SO YOU THINK YOU KNOW ...

FANTASTICAL WORLDS

# Quiz 33

**1.**
What district is Katniss Everdeen from?

**2.**
If you visited Gringotts and Godric's Hollow, whose world would you be in?

**3.**
Who's the queen of Arendelle?

**4.**
Aquaman's mother is from which city?

**5.**
Humans want to mine for the precious metal unobtanium on which moon, home of the Na'vi species?

**6.**
Where is Frodo Baggins from?

**7.**
Superman and Batman inhabit which cities?

**8.**
Who greets Lucy as she stumbles into Narnia, via the back of a wardrobe?

**9.**
The five districts of Fang, Heart, Spine, Talon and Tail, which together make up Kumandra, are from which movie?

**10.**
Which superhero is from Themyscira, home of the Amazons?

# SO YOU THINK
# YOU KNOW ...

# FAMILY
# ADVENTURE

WHAT DO THEY GOT IN THERE, KING KONG?

# Quiz 34

**1.**
Which 2021 action movie was based on a Disney theme park ride?

**2.**
Alan Parrish is a boy who gets stuck inside a game in which 1995 movie?

**3.**
Where does the blood come from that leads to the recreation of dinosaurs in *Jurassic Park*?

**4.**
An FBI agent and an art thief teaming up to catch a criminal is the premise of which 2021 blockbuster?

**5.**
Kevin Costner and Christian Slater play half-brothers in which 90s classic?

**6.**
Which director brought us *Hunt for the Wilderpeople* and *Boy*?

**7.**
What does Guy, the main character in *Free Guy*, surprisingly discover about himself?

**8.**
Ben Stiller is a security guard surrounded by statues that come alive in which movie?

**9.**
Who created a time-traveling machine in a DeLorean car?

**10.**
Sean Connery and Harrison Ford play father and son in which action adventure series?

# SO YOU THINK
# YOU KNOW ...

# MOVIES

# Quiz 35

**1.**
Imperator Furiosa is part of which action franchise?

**2.**
Which epic wartime movie, starring Steve McQueen, Richard Attenborough and Charles Bronson, was based on a true story?

**3.**
Who played the Bosley role in the 2019 *Charlie's Angels* film?

**4.**
Who played Private Ryan in *Saving Private Ryan*?

**5.**
Geena Davis plays an assassin with amnesia in which 90s movie?

**6.**
NYPD detective John McClane is a character in which series of action movies?

**7.**
In which year was the first Fast & Furious movie released?

**8.**
Which two women have played Lara Croft on the big screen?

**9.**
The killing of who puts John Wick on a path to revenge?

**10.**
Ethan Hunt is the protagonist of which series of movies?

# SO YOU THINK YOU KNOW ...

# Quiz 36

**1.**
Jordan Peele made his directorial debut with what movie?

**2.**
Which movie propelled Jennifer Lawrence into the spotlight?

**3.**
Miles Teller is tormented by his teacher, played by J.K. Simmons, in which 2014 movie?

**4.**
In what US city is 2017's *Lady Bird* set?

**5.**
Nine-year-old Quvenzhané Wallis received a Best Actress Oscar nomination for her role in which indie movie?

**6.**
Which blockbuster director made *Memento*, about a man with amnesia?

**7.**
Who played the title role in *Frances Ha*?

**8.**
Three film students go chasing a local legend in the woods in which low-budget blockbuster?

**9.**
What is Steve Zissou, played by Bill Murray, on the hunt for in *The Life Aquatic with Steve Zissou*?

**10.**
Timothée Chalamet learned Italian and piano to play the part of Elio in which movie?

# SO YOU THINK
# YOU KNOW ...

## *MUSICIANS*
## *ON SCREEN*

# Quiz 37

**1.**
Which musician was nominated for a Best Supporting Oscar for her role in 2017's *Mudbound*?

**2.**
Which rocker shoots himself in the foot in *Point Break*?

**3.**
Who played the wife of *Hustler* magazine founder Larry Flint in *The People vs. Larry Flint*?

**4.**
Ice Cube starred in which coming-of-age tale, along with Cuba Gooding Jr. and Laurence Fishburne?

**5.**
Mariah Carey starred as a social worker in which 2009 movie?

**6.**
Justin Timberlake portrayed which real-life person in *The Social Network*?

**7.**
Which singer played NASA engineer Mary Jackson in *Hidden Figures*?

**8.**
Which musician starred in *The Rocky Horror Picture Show*, *Wayne's World* and *Fight Club*?

**9.**
*Blue Hawaii* and *Fun in Acapulco* both star which singer turned actor?

**10.**
Which boy band member starred in which 2017 World War II epic?

# SO YOU THINK
# YOU KNOW ...

# *MARTIAL ARTS*

WAx ON, WAx OFF

# Quiz 38

**1.**
Who directed the movie *Crouching Tiger, Hidden Dragon*?

**2.**
Which movie franchise, adapted from a video game about a martial arts battle for the universe, was rebooted in 2021?

**3.**
Which American movie star founded his own martial art called Chun Kuk Do?

**4.**
Which actor portrayed Mr. Miyagi in *The Karate Kid*?

**5.**
Who wrote, directed and starred in *The Way of the Dragon*?

**6.**
Which two actors play estranged brothers facing off in a mixed martial arts competition in 2011's *Warrior*?

**7.**
Brandon Lee was accidentally killed on the set of which movie?

**8.**
Superstar musician Kylie Minogue starred in which martial arts movie?

**9.**
Chan Kong-sang is the birth name of which Hong Kong–born martial arts star?

**10.**
Jet Li and Aaliyah teamed up in which movie about feuding families?

# SO YOU THINK
# YOU KNOW ...

# FILM
# MOVEMENTS

# Quiz 39

**1.**
What European genre heavily influenced the emergence of Film Noir movies?

**2.**
Which movement, started by Danish directors Lars von Trier and Thomas Vinterberg, places the emphasis on story and performance, shunning expensive special effects?

**3.**
Parallel Cinema is a film movement founded in what country?

**4.**
Which decade saw French Impressionism in film hit its peak?

**5.**
*Battleship Potemkin* is an example of which Russian film movement?

**6.**
*Picnic at Hanging Rock*, *Mad Max* and *Puberty Blues* are examples of which Australian film movement?

**7.**
What film-editing technique was popularized in the French New Wave classic *Breathless*?

**8.**
What movement emerged after World War II, focusing on the Italian poor and working class?

**9.**
The 2003 movie *Oldboy*, remade by Spike Lee in 2013, is an example of which film movement?

**10.**
*Shaft* (1971) and *Superfly* (1972) are examples of which 1970s genre?

# SO YOU THINK
# YOU KNOW ...

# FROM
# STAGE TO
# SCREEN

# Quiz 40

**1.**
Which play, then film, is about an elderly white woman and her African-American chauffeur?

**2.**
Colonel Jessup and Daniel Kaffee are characters in which Aaron Sorkin play that became a movie?

**3.**
True or false: The leads in *Frost/Nixon*, Michael Sheen and Frank Langella, were in the original play?

**4.**
Which rom com began as a one-woman show about the perils of introducing your boyfriend to your large family?

**5.**
Meryl Streep stars as a nun in the 2008 screen version of which play?

**6.**
Which 1963 play became a 1966 movie with Michael Caine in the title role?

**7.**
Daniel Day-Lewis and Winona Ryder starred in a 1996 adaptation of which Arthur Miller play?

**8.**
Which 1957 courtroom drama, based on a play by Reginald Rose, starred Henry Fonda?

**9.**
Which play, then movie, was about blind and deaf Helen Keller and her life-long teacher and companion Anne Sullivan?

**10.**
Which movie starring Paul Newman and Elizabeth Taylor was based on a Tennessee Williams play?

# MOVIE ZOMBIES

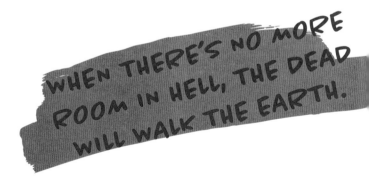

WHEN THERE'S NO MORE ROOM IN HELL, THE DEAD WILL WALK THE EARTH.

# Quiz 41

**1.**
Which often shirtless pop icon plays a member of the undead in *The Dead Don't Die*?

**2.**
Which movie sees the main character waking up after a coma, to the empty streets of London?

**3.**
Bruce Campbell, playing Ash Williams, is the protagonist of which zombie series?

**4.**
Nicholas Hoult plays a zombie in love in which 2013 movie?

**5.**
Model turned actor, Milla Jovovich, heads up which zombie franchise based on a Japanese video game?

**6.**
*Dawn of the Dead* was the sequel of which genre-defining zombie flick?

**7.**
Which 2016 South Korean movie is about a father and daughter fending off zombies on a train?

**8.**
What food snack is Tallahassee, played by Woody Harrelson, on the hunt for in *Zombieland*?

**9.**
Brad Pitt stars as a UN agent trying to find the source of a zombie pandemic in which movie?

**10.**
Which Jane Austen novel has been given a comic zombie makeover?

# SO YOU THINK
# YOU KNOW ...

# WESTERNS

# Quiz 42

**1.**
Which actors played the roles of Butch Cassidy and the Sundance Kid?

**2.**
Atmospheric western thriller *The Power of the Dog* was directed by which Oscar-winning director?

**3.**
What nickname was given to the sub-genre of westerns that were made in Europe?

**4.**
Which 1988 movie featured brothers Emilio Estevez and Charlie Sheen telling the tale of outlaw Billy the Kid?

**5.**
Salma Hayek got her breakout role in which western?

**6.**
What three movies make up Sergio Leone's Dollars trilogy, all starring Clint Eastwood?

**7.**
Which actor known for his western roles was nicknamed the Duke?

**8.**
Jamie Foxx played a freed slave out to save his wife, with the help of a German dentist-come-bounty hunter, in which movie?

**9.**
James Dean's last film role was in which western?

**10.**
What western was Kevin Costner's directorial debut, which he also starred in?

# SO YOU THINK YOU KNOW ...

# Quiz 43

**1.**
The lead in which film has been played by Janet Gaynor, Judy Garland, Barbra Streisand, Shraddha Kapoor and Lady Gaga?

**2.**
Gregory Peck, Martin Balsam and Robert Mitchum cameoed in the remake of which thriller they originally starred in?

**3.**
Brian de Palma directed a remake of which 1932 movie, loosely based on Al Capone?

**4.**
Scarlett Johansson voiced the role of a snake in which 2016 remake of a 1967 movie?

**5.**
Who directed the 2005 remake of *King Kong*?

**6.**
Ricki Lake and Divine played mother and daughter in which musical, remade in 2007 under the same name?

**7.**
George Clooney and Frank Sinatra played which role in the two versions of *Ocean's 11*?

**8.**
*Infernal Affairs*, the 2002 Hong Kong movie, was remade by Martin Scorsese as what movie?

**9.**
The James Bond movie *Thunderball* was remade in 1983 under what title?

**10.**
Which two actors starred as Pennywise in the 1990 mini-series and the 2017 movie version of *It*?

# SO YOU THINK YOU KNOW ...

**COP MOVIES**

# Quiz 44

**1.**
Frances McDormand plays a heavily pregnant police officer in which movie?

**2.**
Who played US Marshall Samuel Gerard in the 1993 film *The Fugitive*?

**3.**
Sandra Bullock gets a glam makeover to take part in which competition in *Miss Congeniality*?

**4.**
What kind of pet does *Kindergarten Cop*'s Arnold Schwarzenegger use to entertain his young charges?

**5.**
What Old Hollywood movie star does Kim Basinger resemble in *L.A. Confidential*?

**6.**
Jodie Foster and Julianne Moore have both played which FBI agent?

**7.**
Which comedic cop caper is the second in Edgar Wright's Three Flavours Cornettos trilogy?

**8.**
Rene Russo played a police officer in which movie franchise?

**9.**
Robert De Niro and Al Pacino face off on opposite sides of the law in which movie?

**10.**
Real-life retired cop Ron Stallworth is played on-screen by John David Washington in which 2018 movie?

## SO YOU THINK
## YOU KNOW ...

# MAKEOVERS

# AND

# BODY SWAPS

# Quiz 45

**1.**
Julia Roberts' character in *Pretty Woman* gets talked down to in a shop on which famous street?

**2.**
In which movie do a boy and girl swap bodies while arguing in front of a statue of an ancient Aztec god?

**3.**
Which two actors swap faces in *Face/Off*?

**4.**
*He's All That* stars which breakout TikTok star?

**5.**
In *Grease*, what does Danny wear to signal he's willing to change to win over Sandy?

**6.**
A 12-year-old boy making a wish to a mechanical fortune-telling machine is the start of which movie?

**7.**
What dance does Jenna, played by Jennifer Garner, do in *13 Going on 30*?

**8.**
What color sweater sparks a withering speech from Miranda Priestly in *The Devil Wears Prada*?

**9.**
Steve Carell's character is made over from daggy to datable in which movie?

**10.**
What triggers mother and daughter to swap bodies in 2006's *Freaky Friday*?

# Answers

**QUIZ 01:** 1. The Lumière brothers 2. Fritz Lang 3. No (it was *A Visit to the Seaside*, 1908) 4. Joan Crawford 5. The Kelly Gang 6. Charlie Chaplin 7. *Snow White and the Seven Dwarfs* 8. 1940s (1946) 9. The Big Five 10. True

**QUIZ 02:** 1. *The Godfather* 2. *The Untouchables* 3. *The Irishman* 4. They are father and son, James and Michael Gandolfini 5. Russell Crowe and Denzel Washington 6. *Goodfellas* 7. *Once Upon a Time in America* 8. *On the Waterfront* 9. Michelle Pfeiffer 10. The Kray twins, Ronnie and Reggie

**QUIZ 03:** 1. Batman 2. X-Men 3. Shazam 4. The Wicked Witch of the East 5. The Joker 6. Hell Boy 7. Catwoman 8. Gene Hackman 9. Maleficent 10. Scott Pilgrim

**QUIZ 04:** 1. Meg Ryan and Tom Hanks 2. She has short-term memory loss 3. Greece 4. *Moonstruck* 5. Bridget Jones 6. *Always Be My Maybe* 7. *10* 8. John Corbett 9. Date doctor/ matchmaker 10. *Pretty Woman* and *Runaway Bride*

**QUIZ 05:** 1. "You Never Can Tell" 2. Ennio Morricone 3. *Do the Right Thing* 4. John Williams 5. Dolly Parton 6. "Lust for Life" by Iggy Pop 7. *Saturday Night Fever* 8. *Selma* 9. *A Clockwork Orange* 10. "Lose Yourself"

**QUIZ 06:** 1. False – both movies are based on the same book 2. *Prometheus* 3. Bill Pullman 4. *Inception* 5. H.G. Wells 6. 2019 and 2049 7. Red 8. Andy Serkis 9. *Tron* 10. Bill and Ted

**QUIZ 07:** 1. *In Cold Blood* 2. Italy 3. Margaret Mitchell 4. *The Color Purple* 5. *Pride and Prejudice* 6. Red 7. Stephen King 8. *12 Years a Slave* 9. Michael Crichton 10. *To Kill a Mockingbird*

**QUIZ 08:** 1. *Fantastic Mr. Fox* 2. Kobe Bryant 3. An onion 4. King Louie the orangutan 5. Elsa 6. Japan 7. Four 8. *Yellow Submarine* 9. Jack Skellington aka the Pumpkin King of Halloween Town 10. New York

**QUIZ 09:** 1. Donald Trump 2. The same jumper and hat worn by Freddy Krueger 3. Keith Richards 4. Marvel creator Stan Lee 5. Director, Peter Jackson 6. Backstreet Boys

7. A TV reporter 8. Glenn
Close 9. George Harrison
10. David Bowie

**QUIZ 10:** 1. *Much Ado
About Nothing* 2. Gwyneth
Paltrow 3. Verona Beach
4. *Hamlet* 5. Gus Van Sant
6. *Macbeth* 7. *The Taming
of the Shrew* 8. Sir John
Gielgud 9. Mark Antony
10. Maria (Juliet) doesn't die

**QUIZ 11:** 1. Count Orlok
2. Razor blades 3. *Scream,
Blacula Scream* 4. *The Lost
Boys* 5. *Let the Right One In*
6. Luke Perry 7. *Underworld*
8. Aaliyah 9. Their skin
sparkles 10. Kirsten Dunst

**QUIZ 12:** 1. McDonald's
fast food 2. *When We Were
Kings* 3. Morgan Freeman
4. *Paris Is Burning* 5. The
Twin Towers of the World
Trade Center in NYC
6. *Searching for Sugar Man*
7. Michael Moore 8. Al Gore
9. *Apocalypse Now* 10. *Exit
Through the Gift Shop*

**QUIZ 13:** 1. Indian Beach,
Oregon, USA 2. Katz's Deli
3. Namibia 4. Central Park
5. *Star Wars* (episodes VII,
VIII and IX) 6. New Zealand
7. Thailand 8. Tunisia 9. Los
Angeles 10. Philadelphia
Museum of Art

**QUIZ 14:** 1. *Manhunter,
The Silence of the Lambs,
Hannibal, Red Dragon,
Hannibal Rising* 2. *The
Fugitive* 3. Bette Davis and
Joan Crawford 4. Roger
"Verbal" Kint 5. *Deliverance*
6. *Single White Female*
7. *Gone Girl* 8. A pet rabbit
9. She breaks his ankles
with a sledgehammer
10. M. Night Shyamalan

**QUIZ 15:** 1. *12 Years
a Slave* 2. *Jaws* 3. *Star
Wars V: The Empire
Strikes Back* 4. *A League
of Their Own* 5. *Meet the
Parents* 6. *Mean Girls*
7. *Citizen Kane* 8. *Labyrinth*
9. *Legally Blonde* 10. *It's a
Wonderful Life*

**QUIZ 16:** 1. Nuclear
radiation 2. Never feed it
after midnight 3. Gwoemul
4. Balrog 5. Critters
6. Small children 7. Adam/
The Creature, from *Mary
Shelley's Frankenstein*
8. *Creature from the Black
Lagoon* 9. Make a noise
10. *King Kong*

**QUIZ 17:** 1. Live baby eels
2. Italy 3. White Russian
4. A giant chocolate cake
5. Whisky (Suntory) 6. A
stick of gum 7. Cubanos
(Cuban pork sandwiches)
8. Breakfast strata 9. Fried
green tomatoes 10. Fava
beans and a nice Chianti

**QUIZ 18:** 1. *Iron Man*,
2008 2. T'Challa
3. To help fight in World
War II 4. Strategic
Homeland Intervention,
Enforcement and Logistics
Division 5. Wanda Maximoff
and Vision 6. No (Thor
is an Asgardian and
Loki is a Frost Giant of
Jotunn descent) 7. False –
Cooper voices Rocket,
and Vin Diesel voices
Groot 8. *Avengers*,
2012 9. Neurosurgeon
10. Simu Liu

**QUIZ 19:** 1. None – Adonis
is the son of Rocky's foe
turned friend, Apollo Creed
2. Venus and Serena
Williams 3. *Chariots of Fire*
4. Tonya Harding
5. A baseball field, the
ghosts of legendary
baseballers 6. Tallulah
7. The Melbourne Cup
8. *Raging Bull* 9. Billie Jean
King 10. Roller derby

**QUIZ 20:** 1. Jemaine
Clement and Taika
Waititi 2. *Jennifer's Body*
3. *Scary Movie* 4. Animals
5. Jennifer Aniston
6. *Tusk* 7. Venus flytrap
8. *Beetlejuice* 9. *Drag
Me To Hell* 10. *Happy
Death Day*

**QUIZ 21:** 1. It must feature two women who talk to each other about something other than a man 2. True 3. Alison Bechdel 4. *The Simpsons* 5. Sweden 6. *Thelma and Louise* 7. A comic strip 8. 1985 9. They never speak to each other 10. All three

**QUIZ 22:** 1. *Mamma Mia!* 2. *Grease* 3. Fabulous Godmother 4. Seven 5. *Cabaret* 6. Siam (Thailand) 7. Lin-Manuel Miranda 8. *South Pacific* 9. *My Fair Lady* 10. Queen Latifa

**QUIZ 23:** 1. *Rear Window* 2. Daphne du Maurier 3. Anthony Perkins 4. Cary Grant 5. *A Perfect Murder* 6. Suspense 7. *Rope* 8. Golden Gate Bridge 9. Tippi Hedren 10. Three (*Dial M for Murder*, *Rear Window*, *To Catch a Thief*)

**QUIZ 24:** 1. 1953 2. *Moonlight* 3. Most nominations for acting without a win (both nominated eight times) 4. An egg 5. Marlon Brando 6. *Parasite* 7. World War II (there was a metal shortage) 8. *Ben-Hur*, *Titanic*, *Lord of the Rings: Return of the*

*King* 9. Kathryn Bigelow, *The Hurt Locker*, 2008 10. Bob Hope

**QUIZ 25:** 1. Tilda Swinton 2. Tom Marvolo Riddle 3. *The Craft* 4. *Fantasia* 5. Gandalf 6. *Excalibur* 7. *Practical Magic* 8. Snakes 9. *Hocus Pocus* 10. Three – although we only see the feet of one of them

**QUIZ 26:** 1. Jean Paul Gaultier 2. Blue gingham 3. Tom Ford 4. *The Seven Year Itch* 5. *Clueless* 6. Red 7. *A Clockwork Orange* 8. Halle Berry 9. Green 10. Anna Wintour, editor in chief of US *Vogue*

**QUIZ 27:** 1. Angela Bassett and Laurence Fishburne 2. *Straight Outta Compton* 3. *My Left Foot* 4. Freddie Mercury 5. Harvey Milk 6. Ruth Bader Ginsburg 7. Locked-in syndrome 8. NASA 9. *Into the Wild* 10. Diana Ross

**QUIZ 28:** 1. 1977 2. Dagobah 3. X-wing 4. Four (episodes IV, I, II and III) 5. Billy Dee Williams and Donald Glover 6. His father, Darth Vader 7. Emperor Palpatine 8. Princess Leia 9. Padmé Amidala and Anakin Skywalker (Darth Vader) 10. Ewok

**QUIZ 29:** 1. Lassie 2. Babe 3. Rex Harrison, Eddie Murphy and Robert Downey Jr. 4. A giant anaconda 5. Hedwig 6. *Free Willy* 7. Bengal Tiger, spotted hyena, orangutan, zebra 8. Labrador Retriever 9. Snakes 10. *Arachnophobia*

**QUIZ 30:** 1. Freddy Krueger 2. William Shatner 3. Journalist 4. *When a Stranger Calls* 5. A Good Guys Doll 6. A hook 7. Friday the 13th 8. *Texas Chainsaw Massacre* 9. *Freddy vs. Jason* 10. *Slumber Party Massacre*

**QUIZ 31:** 1. Potatoes 2. *Apollo 13* 3. Moon 4. *Spaceballs* 5. *Alien* 6. Benedict Cumberbatch 7. They worked drilling for oil in the ocean 8. *Gravity* 9. *Contact* 10. True: 88 of the 161 minutes are dialogue-free

**QUIZ 32:** 1. Sean Connery, George Lazenby, Roger Moore, Timothy Dalton, Pierce Brosnan, Daniel Craig 2. Fat Bastard 3. Johnny English 4. *Hanna* 5. *Argo* 6. Guy Ritchie 7. Kingsman 8. Five-point palm exploding heart technique 9. *Salt* 10. *La Femme Nikita*

**QUIZ 33:** 1. District 12
2. Harry Potter's 3. Elsa
4. Atlantis 5. Pandora
6. The Shire 7. Metropolis
and Gotham City
8. Mr. Tumnus 9. *Raya and the Last Dragon* 10. Wonder Woman aka Diana of Themyscira/Diana Prince

**QUIZ 34:** 1. *Jungle Cruise*
2. *Jumanji* 3. From a mosquito trapped in amber
4. *Red Notice* 5. *Robin Hood: Prince of Thieves*
6. Taika Waititi 7. That he's a non-player character in an online game 8. *Night at the Museum* 9. Emmett "Doc" Brown 10. Indiana Jones

**QUIZ 35:** 1. Mad Max
2. *The Great Escape*
3. Patrick Stewart 4. Matt Damon 5. *The Long Kiss Goodnight* 6. Die Hard
7. 2001 8. Angelina Jolie and Alicia Vikander
9. Daisy, his puppy
10. Mission Impossible

**QUIZ 36:** 1. *Get Out*
2. *Winter's Bone*
3. *Whiplash* 4. Sacramento, California 5. *Beasts of the Southern Wild*
6. Christopher Nolan
7. Greta Gerwig 8. *The Blair Witch Project* 9. A shark that ate his friend 10. *Call Me By Your Name*

**QUIZ 37:** 1. Mary J. Blige
2. Anthony Kiedis
3. Courtney Love 4. *Boyz n the Hood* 5. *Precious*
6. Sean Parker 7. Janelle Monae 8. Meatloaf 9. Elvis Presley 10. Harry Styles, *Dunkirk*

**QUIZ 38:** 1. Ang Lee
2. Mortal Kombat 3. Chuck Norris 4. Noriyuki "Pat" Morita 5. Bruce Lee 6. Joel Edgerton and Tom Hardy
7. *The Crow* 8. *Street Fighter* 9. Jackie Chan
10. *Romeo Must Die*

**QUIZ 39:** 1. German Expressionism 2. Dogme 95
3. India 4. 1920s 5. Soviet Montage 6. Australian New Wave 7. Jump cut 8. Italian neorealism 9. Korean New Wave 10. Blaxploitation

**QUIZ 40:** 1. *Driving Miss Daisy* 2. *A Few Good Men*
3. True 4. *My Big Fat Greek Wedding* 5. *Doubt* 6. *Alfie*
7. *The Crucible* 8. *12 Angry Men* 9. *The Miracle Worker*
10. *Cat on a Hot Tin Roof*

**QUIZ 41:** 1. Iggy Pop
2. *28 Days Later* 3. Evil Dead 4. *Warm Bodies*
5. Resident Evil 6. *Night of the Living Dead* 7. *Train to Busan* 8. Twinkie 9. *World War Z* 10. *Pride and Prejudice*

**QUIZ 42:** 1. Paul Newman and Robert Redford 2. Jane Campion 3. Spaghetti western 4. *Young Guns*
5. *Desperado* 6. *A Fistful of Dollars*, *For a Few Dollars More* and *The Good, the Bad and the Ugly*
7. John Wayne 8. *Django Unchained* 9. *Giant*
10. *Dances with Wolves*

**QUIZ 43:** 1. *A Star Is Born* 2. *Cape Fear*
3. *Scarface* 4. *The Jungle Book* 5. Peter Jackson
6. *Hairspray* 7. Danny Ocean 8. *The Departed*
9. *Never Say Never Again*
10. Tim Curry and Bill Skarsgård

**QUIZ 44:** 1. *Fargo* 2. Tommy Lee Jones 3. Miss United States pageant 4. A ferret
5. Veronica Lake 6. Clarice Starling 7. *Hot Fuzz*
8. Lethal Weapon 9. *Heat*
10. *BlacKkKlansman*

**QUIZ 45:** 1. Rodeo Drive
2. *It's a Boy Girl Thing*
3. John Travolta and Nicolas Cage 4. Addison Rae 5. A letterman sweater
6. *Big* 7. Thriller 8. Cerulean
9. *Crazy, Stupid, Love*
10. A magic fortune cookie

# Smith Street Books

TOTO, I'VE A FEELING WE'RE NOT IN KANSAS ANYMORE

Published in 2022 by Smith Street Books
Naarm | Melbourne | Australia
smithstreetbooks.com

ISBN: 978-1-92275-400-4

Publisher: Paul McNally
Text: Aisling Coughlan
Editor: Ariana Klepac
Designer: Vanessa Masci
Layout: Megan Ellis
Proofreader: Pamela Dunne
Cover illustration: Chantel De Sousa

Printed & bound in China by C&C Offset Printing Co., Ltd.

Book 232
10 9 8 7 6 5 4 3 2 1

MIX
Paper from
responsible sources
FSC® C008047